An Outstretched Hand

An Outstretched Hand

POEMS, PRAYERS, AND MEDITATIONS

ROD McKUEN

CHEVAL BOOKS
LOS ANGELES
New York Johannesburg
Sydney London

HARPER & ROW, PUBLISHERS
SAN FRANCISCO
Cambridge London
Hagerstown Mexico City
Philadelphia São Paulo
New York Sydney

1817

An Outstretched Hand. Copyright © 1980 by Rod McKuen and Montcalm Productions.

Printed in the United States of America.

Published simultaneously in Canada by Fitzhenry & Whiteside, Limited, Toronto.

Acknowledgments on pp. 149–151 are considered a continuation of this copyright page.

FIRST EDITION

Designed by Patricia Girvin Dunbar and Rod McKuen

Library of Congress Cataloging in Publication Data

McKuen, Rod.
    An outstretched hand.

    I. Title.
PS3525.A26409   811'.54   78–20589
ISBN 0–06–250568–8

80   81   82   83   84   10   9   8   7   6   5   4   3   2   1

By Rod McKuen

BOOKS

PROSE
Finding My Father
An Outstretched Hand

POETRY
And Autumn Came
Stanyan Street & Other Sorrows
Listen to the Warm
Lonesome Cities
In Someone's Shadow
Caught in the Quiet
Fields of Wonder
And to Each Season
Come to Me in Silence
Moment to Moment
Celebrations of the Heart
Beyond the Boardwalk
The Sea Around Me
Coming Close to the Earth
We Touch the Sky
The Power Bright and Shining

COLLECTED POEMS
Twelve Years of Christmas
A Man Alone
With Love . . .
The Carols of Christmas
Seasons in the Sun
Alone
The Rod McKuen Omnibus*
Hand in Hand
The Works of Rod McKuen*
Love's Been Good to Me
Looking For A Friend

COLLECTED LYRICS
New Ballads
Pastorale
The Songs of Rod McKuen
Grand Tour

MUSIC COLLECTIONS
The McKuen/Sinatra Song Book

New Ballads
At Carnegie Hall
McKuen/Brel: Collaboration
28 Greatest Hits
Jean and Other Nice Things
McKuen Country
New European Windows
Greatest Hits, Vol. I
Greatest Hits, Vol. II
Children's Song Book

CLASSICAL MUSIC

BALLET
Americana, R.F.D.
Point/Counterpoint
Seven Elizabethan Dances
The Minotaur (Man to Himself)
Volga Song
Full Circle
The Plains of My Country
Dance Your Ass Off

OPERA AND CHORAL MUSIC
The Black Eagle
Fourteen New Christmas Carols

CONCERTOS
For Piano & Orchestra
For Cello & Orchestra
For Orchestra & Voice
For Guitar & Orchestra
#2 for Piano & Orchestra
For Four Harpsichords

SYMPHONIES & SYMPHONIC SUITES
Symphony #1
Symphony #2
Ballad of Distances
The City
Symphony #3

*Available only in Great Britain

I wish to express my gratitude to Lt. Comdr. William L. Perry, Chaplain, U.S.N., and Art Carson for suggestions on material to include in this book; to Jane Campbell and Jane Gaither for long ago starting me in the right direction; to Father Marlin Bowman, Father Millard Streeter, and John Damm, who came into my life at the right times; to Nan Talese, my original editor on *Listen to the Warm, Twelve Years of Christmas, Pastorale, The Carols of Christmas, The Sea Around Me, Lonesome Cities,* and other volumes from which some of this material was taken; to Rebecca Greer from *Woman's Day* for continued encouragement; to Richard Shack for prodding; to Helen Brann for understanding; to Pamela Burns for tender love and care; and special thanks to Clayton Carlson for his help emotionally, intellectually, and editorially. Finally, anything I write that has to do with my spiritual beliefs owes its beginnings to my mother.

CONTENTS

This book is for Sister Mark Sandy, a continual inspiration to me and to all those fortunate enough to know her.

An Outstretched Hand

Each of us was made by God
and some of us grew tall.
Others stood out in the wind
their branches bent and fell.
Those of us who walk in light
must help the ones in darkness up.
For that's what life is all about
and love is all there is to life.

Each of us was made by God
beautiful in His mind's eye.
Those of us who turned out sound
should look across our shoulders once
and help the weak ones to their feet.

It only takes an outstretched hand.

from Lonesome Cities, *1968*

INTRODUCTION

This book's title, *An Outstretched Hand*, is meant to suggest what I believe to be the two most important ideas in our lives—that God continually waits to take us by the hand and help us reach His Kingdom, and that as His sons and daughters, we must keep our hands and arms outstretched to one another in friendship and love.

In taking the risk of writing on such personal topics as moral, ethical, and religious beliefs, an author should be as direct and clear as possible—as honest with himself as he can be, but still elastic enough to ignite the reader's imagination. No two of us are alike, and what I believe won't necessarily work for you. But however any of us arrives at Christian doctrine there are certain rules, truths, and obligations that are common to all of us.

Three principles of belief are important to me. The first is that there are many ways to reach God. The second is that none of us can really chart the course for another; we can only help by sharing our ideas and beliefs as illustrations, never as definitive roadmaps. The third is that we must be allowed, and allow ourselves, to grow and continually to change. As a part of our humanness, we spend a whole lifetime redefining our beliefs. Very often the changes deepen, add to, or amplify our previous beliefs. Sometimes they take a new direction altogether. In either case, it is necessary for me to see belief as a continual and ever-unfolding process.

Those who know my work are keenly aware that I have jousted with, collided against, and gone seeking God often. This, then, is a testament of my journey so far. In the beginning I was motivated by selfishness, but lately I have forced myself to think more and more about God; and so much has recently happened to me that I can't help feeling God must be doing some extensive thinking about me. So maybe it has not been a forced examination after all.

One thing should be made clear: I have not been "born again," in the currently popular use of that phrase. At least not yet. I do not consider myself a fundamentalist Christian, though what I have written here contains what I believe are the fundamental rules for being a practicing Christian.

I feel, for example, that belief in God is central to belief in life itself. If you believe the wind blows, the sun rises and sets, that there are good people and people who, in the final analysis, are so difficult that you have to move along to where you can be of better use, you must also believe in God. It's just that God is not so tangible. You can't take Him by the hand or point Him out to your friends. God is an attitude, a suggestion, a way of life, and aside from the very small reason for our being here, God is the reason for anything to be and the cause for all being.

My God is not a man of fire and brimstone. He is not some white-haired old man in the sky. I do not see Him hovering over churches on Sunday. Though

I think about God a lot, no incantations will bring that face in front of me, no amount of praying will save me from the troubles that I, myself, create. I have said that God manifests Himself in the good things we do for one another. I continue to believe that, but I believe more.

God can be likened to a father watching over us, but one who has limited His action on our behalf—encouraging us to stand alone and to learn that we can handle with grace and dignity whatever trouble, discouragement, loss, or pain is inflicted on us. He knows success is earned in Christian life, not given as a badge of merit. That's what this book is meant to be about.

Of course God continually watches over us. He is always there to take care of us. But it seems to me we should do more meditating on behalf of others and the good he has provided for the world at large instead of always invoking his name on airplane trips for our own safe passage, or for many of the trivial and selfish needs we can work out for ourselves. After all, he did give us the equipment to solve the majority of our own problems. By all means when trouble comes we should go to him, but more prayers should be offered in thanksgiving than for handouts. Too often we forget just how much he gives us to be thankful for.

Each section of *An Outstretched Hand* contains a statement of intent, followed by a series of meditations, poems, and prayers. The work ends with a series of questions I have asked and tried to answer for myself. I include them because the process of asking and then struggling for answers helped me. I hope it may prove of some value to others.

Most of the thoughts contained here are new, at least for me; others now seem obvious and make me wonder why I waited to share them. A few poems and meditations are from previously published books and public statements, some in their original form and some amended for this book. All of what I have to say within these pages is offered in a spirit of thanksgiving and hope—thanksgiving for the freedom to say them and hope that a line, or even a sentence between the lines, will be of some help to the reader on his or her own life's journey.

I am not a prophet or a teacher. I offer this collection as one human being to another. It is my way of responding to the many hands that have been outstretched to me in my own life.

R.M.
March, 1980

STARTING
BY BELIEVING

Without belief in God, it is more difficult
for us to believe in ourselves.

Accepting God

There, inside a shadow. Intangible amid the morning or the evening mist. Beyond the wall. Behind the half-closed door or within the wood that hides the field and beyond the wood . . . more likely just before our own perception of Him, God waits with an outstretched hand to help us through the shadows, past the mists, and over and beyond the walls we build to keep Him out. He is less a mystery than we make of Him, as all things spiritual are easier than we suppose when we finally try with truth and work to penetrate them.

Our failure to find God—and remember it is our failure, not His, for He continually clears the path that leads us out of ourselves to Him—lies in our inability to perceive Him and His work. This is not just because of our laziness in studying the Scriptures, or our difficulty in following the example of people who have had their lives changed by finding and following their Maker. It is born of our unwillingness to believe in anything except that which we can touch and smell and see.

And yet we believe in airplanes, x-rays, the atom, radio, the telephone, people speaking to us from television sets and movie screens, and rockets to distant planets. It is true that scientific explanations are available for all these phenomena, but few of us seek them out or demand firsthand details. In the end, most of us merely believe. Why not believe in God?

No one asks us to depend on blind faith as proof of God's existence. Daily miracles surround us as proof that He not only exists but is a working God who, hour by hour, rearranges the day and gives continued reason for our being.

I believe a blade of grass is no less a miracle than an airplane. Lightning and follow-the-leader thunder are as powerful for me as rocket ships. Having sailed balloons through the lower heavens and seen the glories of creation, Alexander Graham Bell's telephone holds no special magic for me.

Why do I believe in God? Because there has to be an architect and master builder for all things, even for scientists and inventors. For me, this means no scientist has yet been able to explain scientists.

We are here. An undeniable fact, but a fact filled with mystery. Without that original mystery, there would be no need for scientists. True, without science we would have no explanation for why one human being is different from another, why differences exist within the same species of animal, and why plant life browns and seemingly dies, only to regenerate itself according to the season. But the birth of a child and the birth of a butterfly would still be magic absolute, with or without science and its practitioners.

Making each of us different, yet with the same inherent capabilities for good and evil, was probably God's most valuable and exciting gift to us. He wanted us to find our own way in the world and to find our way to Him. This life is but a test. Each of us must show our worthiness for whatever is to come later.

We are familiar with birth, life, death, but what about the Christian belief in the life hereafter? To the first three we continually bear witness, but the fourth is difficult—and for some, impossible—to imagine or believe, because those who have experienced the moment on the deathbed, the battlefield, or just before the coffin closes, have left us no record of the sight, the feel, or the smell of the Holy Spirit as it waits to welcome the soul of the dead or dying to meet the outstretched hand of God. That we must accept on faith.

As Christians we are not asked to accept *everything* on faith, but without faith we would have no Christianity at all. Since Christian belief is based almost equally upon faith and doctrine, we must use both as tools to help us understand what God expects of us as individuals, and why mysteries—such as the Holy Spirit—must remain mysteries. God and those things He chooses to have remain His secrets are not easy to understand, but as we grow older we learn that the study of His reasons for keeping things a mystery is a special reward in itself.

Questions unasked remain unanswered. Mysteries not looked into will continue to stay locked away. God welcomes questions as He welcomes prayers. It is unlikely any of us will ever ascertain all the secrets surrounding Him, though God becomes less misunderstood and less mysterious the more we examine His doctrines and attempt to imitate the life of His Son, Jesus Christ.

Rich man, pauper, priest—God does not choose His children by station, situation, or vocation. Because He is the Maker of all things, His capacity for compassion encompasses everyone. God does not favor the greedy, the dishonest, the cruel and vicious, nor is he fond of liars, those who steal, those who fail to keep His commandments. But He turns His back on no one. A man of greed who learns charity is welcome in God's sight. The murderer and the liar, truly repentant, are able to seek and receive forgiveness. I truly believe God lets us make mistakes as part of our growth. He does not steer us into darkness but is always there to guide us into light. What we must do is be willing to come out from the shadows into God's illumination.

Surely a God intelligent enough to give us so much complexity must know our lives can be made more meaningful by realizing that we are part of His family, that despite our diversities we can learn some simple truths by being at one with Him. Whether or not we accept our duties and responsibilities as family members is up to us.

It is impossible to put too much stress on the importance of this life. Living means continually earning the right to be here. Life, with all its excitement and exasperation, is something we should strive to make less complicated every day. And as women and men created by God and for His glory, we need each other's help to make our lives work. Though we may never reach the ultimate goal in life—simplicity—each of us must try to make his or her life as uncluttered as possible. Only then do we deserve our place on earth. Only then are we equipped to give and to accept love. Only then can we be willing friends, holding nothing back from those we care about, sharing everything and expecting nothing in return.

But I am not sure even this is enough to earn an afterlife for us. It may be that one can place too much importance on what comes after this life ends. Though we should continually prepare for the time our earthly bodies become unnecessary and our souls take over, it is doubtful that many of us *will* be ready. Believers have to keep restating their beliefs and re-defining them; only in so doing can they come upon the real joy of discovery. And continuing revelation brings heaven closer to hand.

God did not intend us to be marionettes manipulated by Him. We have, therefore, so much to learn about Christian living that whether we are converted at the cradle or the deathbed, we will never have time enough to fully mature as perfected children of God.

It is important, however, to remember that God means for each of us to *try*. In the Bible, God's disciples do not claim to be *holy men*, purged from sin, but each works toward that state of grace. The expression *I'll die trying*, used so often and so offhandedly, ought to be the Christian's motto.

Recently, a friend confessed to me that at age thirty his life was one-third over and he still didn't have a fix on what he wanted to do with his remaining years. I am a good deal older than my friend, and yet I, too, wonder if I'm doing the right thing or will ever learn my capabilities, let alone expand them. Still, I refuse not to accept each day as an opportunity for discovery, or at least a challenge and a chance for change.

I have tried many organized religions and not always come away satisfied with their doctrine, but I have been continually amazed and pleased with the many people I met who, like me, were still searching. I have never gone to a religious organization or prayer meeting, Sunday School, or church in search of God. I have always felt that God *is*. If He exists in Sunday School or at a Mass, He is no less present during a business meeting, a shopping trip, or even when I feel most alone. This does not mean that I advocate doing away with church attendance. It can be a meaningful spiritual and social necessity for many Christians.

Once, a well-meaning godfather, who decided my not attending church was becoming an alarming habit, sent a priest to my house in an attempt at rescue. I liked the man, and we talked a long time. Finally, he gave me what I consider the best reason anyone ever had for attending an organized church on a regular basis: "We are too much into ourselves," he said. "Once a week it's good to get out of our selfish selves and dwell on something else, preferably God. Attending a service where other people have come to seek God creates a more workable climate for finding Him." That was more than twenty years ago. His reasoning is even more important now, particularly in the current climate of thought that puts *self* above everything else.

The quest is not to seek out God, for He is everywhere. Rather, it is to learn more about Him. In so doing we expand our capabilities and increase our knowledge of ourselves. Accepting God, then, is finally coming to accept ourselves.

Do not be afraid to dream. Dreamers who put their thoughts into deeds and actions become God's leaders here on earth. As the visible world is sustained by the invisible, so humanity, stripped of its trials, sins, and sordid vocations, is nourished by the beautiful visions of its solitary dreams. Humanity cannot forget those dreams, because it lives by them—and God surely has reserved a special place in heaven for dreamers who have helped their fellow human beings.

April

April is the only time we need not ask God for miracles or transformations. They come unsolicited from everywhere. He sends them to us without prayer or limitations.

Tulips and the birth of grass, morning-glories in the morning and lilacs all day long, April holds us so firm that we could swear the screech owl's singing was a choir of nightingales paid to serenade the neighborhood like a touring minstrel band.

April is the tuning fork for the spring and summer months ahead, and God is everywhere—and home.

Amen should be abolished from the end of prayers—
since praise of God should be a lifelong prayer
whether uttered in silence or aloud.

In God we find reality and reason. Without the
quest for God there is no quest at all. Because be-
lief in Him provides the only perfect balance in our
lives, to deny Him is to withhold a part of ourselves
from ourselves and all others to whom we feel
close.

God is gotten to by work, not walking.

Our relationship with God is the most secure to
be found on earth or within the cosmos.

Let no one presume to write your history . . . live it.
And any man who can prove to you conclusively
the absence of God from the universe must surely
be a god himself.

Hold onto your visions. Cherish your ideals. Do not be afraid of the music and poetry that stirs within your heart or the beauty that forms in your mind, for—if you nurture them, care for them, and remain true to their original concepts—out of them will grow heavenly environments. Remember that if we come from God, so do all our dreams and actions, even those actions and thoughts that shame us in the sunlight. Think about it: it should not be difficult to think good thoughts and dream only those dreams that, put into action, make life better not just for yourself but for all of God's children.

While traversing our lifetimes, we should not take steps that lead us year to year or even day to decade, only moment to moment.

God is love—in Him we find the reason for all love. The need for love—not just from other human beings, but from God Himself. The necessity to offer love to our friends, our would-be enemies, and to all things He created—even when we come upon adversity.

If you want to find truth, you have to look for it . . . but be patient, nothing beautiful comes too easy.

Flying in the Face of God

In a biplane once while flying higher than I thought I could, I half expected to meet God behind each cloud I passed. God with the face of Father Christmas would be smiling or frowning with a frown I bet I knew.

We didn't meet but that is not to say we didn't touch or that we didn't pass by close.

I have the courage now to one day fly through air so thin only God could live there with any certainty.

If I fall back down again a hand of sure direction will have pushed me.

If God exists, He exists for everybody.

When you conquer fear, you conquer failure. How many times you fail or succeed in your own mind is not as important in the eyes of God as how many times you *try.*

To conquer the fear of failing you need only remain open and willing to succeed.

It's a hard road if you've known one better, but a soft rain if you've had one wetter.

Why is it we are, all of us, brave enough to follow any road we're offered, no matter how mysterious, and yet we are fearful and unwilling, day by day in our actions and our prayers, to investigate and then hike down the only true highway?

Although Christ is our confidant, our counselor and comrade, try not to bore Him with unimportant prayers.

Pray to God for your own salvation but don't forget that of your friends, for when the time comes for Him to take you in His arms and lead you beyond this life into a more useful one, the reunion of loved ones who have the same spiritual direction and dedication will be a celebration in itself.

It is wrong not to love, for God made so much in the world deserving of our ardor.

Bell Ringers

Does the bell ring truly
for all and each of us
or does the bell clang only
when the rope is pulled
                    by others?
Ringers of the bell,
              tollers,
bell ringers all,
why do you peal the bell?
Nothing changes
by its ringing.

Unless by chance
the bells are truly
rung by God.
Perhaps He hears us then
perhaps He smiles
and finds the clanging
                booming music
to His liking.

I hope that's so
I hope each candle
         lit for Him
or our own guilt
helps to light His dinner table.

As for bells,
I pray that He hears music
waltzes, tangoes, lilting songs
that make the walks
amid His house
and through His gardens
as beautiful as He
strings out the night for us
and lights up
most our mornings.

The more we share, the more we can truly call our own. Giving returns so much to us it can almost be termed an act of selfishness.

When I think about the distance to doubt, I find it too far to go.

There is little time within the day for one who watches everything and everyone. Even God must tire. Go easily this day. Some of us will try to do without You for an hour, even knowing that we can't.

Why is it we fear age? Time makes us wiser, it strips away our false impressions of ourselves and others, it even makes us more compassionate toward our fellow human beings. Best of all, growing older brings us closer to God; for as we age our perceptions of what's right for us grow clearer and our spiritual needs better defined.

A prayer at its best is part of a conversation with God, and if the other voice remains silent it is because God's conversations are made up of doing, not talking.

Only when we pause to wonder do we go beyond the limits of our little lives.

It is harder to disbelieve than to believe in God. Our intelligence and sensibility point out so many miracles around us every day that to ignore or doubt God's hand in all things is nearly impossible.

Beyond each hill a new one waits and pulls us like the hidden hands of love.

It is not possible to put too much emphasis on prayer. Prayers should become a habit like eating and sleeping and taking care of our brothers and sisters. But the prayer should not be mouthed from something learned within the Scriptures or taught by preachers, pastors, or so-called wise men. A prayer, to be an honest offering to God, should be made up differently each time.

Two Prayers of Acceptance

I accept You, God, not only as my personal savior, but as the giver and the taker of all life. And so my life is Yours. I will be careful with my life, because I only live it with Your good grace. I will work to please You. Tell me of Your needs and I will make them mine.

Almighty God, give me Your strength. I believe in Your strength, and I will use it not for selfish reasons, but for Your glory. Almighty God, give me some measure of Your understanding, that I might know myself better so that I can work for You.

THE GIFT OF LIFE

What a joy to be alive and know it.
To yell from a hilltop or out a window,
I'm here, and really know it.

The House We Live In

We celebrate the giver of life. The maker. He makes all seasons turn. The builder of the world and the inventor of woman and of man, together for each other's needs and at each other's side.

All things wild. The bird that flies on sure or hesitating wings. Eagle, hawk, snowbird, sparrow. Hummingbird upon the backyard vine, the bee within the overlapping leaves of the hollyhock.

The bull that rules the barnyard. The dog that stalks the cat. The cat that ferrets out the mouse. The squirrel that robs the oak. The raccoon that robs the squirrel. The oak, the bushes, and the green-brown grass that hides them all.

The springs that spring from nowhere. The oceans that encircle us. The brook, the stream, the widest river. The rapids and the tidal wave. The dew upon the lawn, the cold that ices pond and lake. The thaw that sets the world in motion yet again.

The silence and the thunder. The lightning and the flint. The gentle rain, the flood. The well that must be pumped, the waterfall that flows forever.

The otter, whale, and dolphin. The skittish fish and friendly fish, the unseen families beneath the sea. Guardians there should be of everything that sails or swims the ocean.

All the oceans land to land, God gave to us and placed in trust for us.

He made the mountains mountainous, the hills an easy climb. The air we breathe, the way in which we take it in and let it out. Clouds that glide and those that billow. The stars that we set out to reach, the skyway leading back. The sky as highway to Him.

Every tree and every turning vine, plants that seem to pop up through the ground and those that spring from roots, the porcupine and porcupine-like cactus, the polar bear, the poplar tree, the willow. The brown bear slicing hives in search of honey; the caterpillar measuring its world until its transformation into powdered moth or pretty butterfly. A Bible could not delineate, a printing press would die in dust before the names of all things made during that one week of creation could be listed.

The inchworm, the anaconda. The house spider, the squid. The tea rose and the rows on rows of poppies, Indian paint brush and clover in the wilderness.

By whose direction, magic, or logic have we finally determined that beasts are lower than man? Is it possible that our thought process and speech are only *different* from that of animals? It is important to remember God made wild roses, tall trees and scrub pines, great oceans and bodies of land: who are we to presume that these "non-human" *things* were made merely for our pleasure? Yet we continue to destroy great forests, to ruin our streams and rivers with our own excrement and pollution. We trample the grass underfoot as though it were a private carpet. This *matter* we are so careless with is no less the property of God than we are. We ought to be more careful with His dwelling place.

We are the shepherds and guardians, custodians and caretakers of God's wide, round garden. It is a sacred trust for each of us, as God's tenants, to care and take care of His world.

In addition to our role as guardians and good shepherds, we should be the planters of more seeds and shielders of God's wonderful gifts. We could begin by unlearning what we know, the building of fences and the mixing of mortar for walls.

We made the wheel, God didn't. And we have learned more destructive ways to use that wheel than ways to put it to good use.

We must not depend on God to always water His garden. We accept the beauty, but too often avoid the responsibility of its upkeep.

What an amazing place this world is. What a mansion made for us to live in. Every time we think about the world we inherited, we ought to breathe a prayer to God that one day we will all be worthy tenants.

Celebrate!

All creatures living on the earth were made or made up by the living God.

So celebrate the time of animals every time you sing out the holidays of humanity.

I am concerned with all human beings, for they are of my family. No less with the bird that sails on open wing, all things that crawl or climb within my vision and beyond.

If God has truly made this earth for me and my likeness, He must have meant that I should share it with all the others He left here to take up His good space and air.

Thank you, God! Though that must fall strangely on anyone's ears but His, it should be said aloud, and often.

We celebrate You.

In Order of Importance

Bless the children first,
for they need help
just to get them safely
down the block.
With all the mazes
that we make for them
(like teaching them to hate
before they learn to spell)
it's a wonder that they ever find
the door that opens out to adolescence.

Bless the animals
that sniff the kitchen floor
and those that prowl the hills.
Animals, like angels, need protection,
because we use them only
as a substitute for love —
the kind that other people promise us
while they steal our evenings
and before they sneak away.

Sunset Colors

I love the sunset colors not just in spring but every day. Every day that God is good enough to share His red and orange and yellow with me and mine. Lately I sleep late, and so I seldom see the scarlet morning or the gold behind the trees. I depend a lot on sunsets. Even when no sunset comes I fill my head with all the sunshine past and sunsets that I know will come. Looking in your eyes I see the sun come even in the darkness.

Do you know how much I feel for you and in what kind of way? I feel the world for you and in every kind of way. I think sometimes that I'll explode, that I'll die or disappear before I have the chance to tell you how I feel. Don't let it be today.

Go forward, straight ahead. There are no limits on your life but those barricades you build yourself.

Maybe we seek God so we'll have someone to understand us. Or were we conjured up by God so that He might find some understanding in the things he invents and builds?

God isn't just the rainbow, He's the rainbow maker.

We don't begin to grow until we start to take full responsibility for our lives.

Iowa from an Airplane

Above Iowa and looking down
the patchwork quilt of frames
unfolding through the oval window.
Now short green squares,
now broad gray triangles
and oblong stretches
of fresh-turned chocolate earth
that surveyors would find hard
                              to pace off.
Plots and pleats of land
orphaned from a quilting bee.

Though mid-April grapples
              with the middle earth
bare trees still stand bare.
Airports are the only eyesore
as silos dot and red barns dash
                              the land,
and God plays bridge
with unseen friends
and shows the world His hand.

Tractors track the squares
and fences follow crooked lines
              they helped create,
but even fences make no boundaries
and Iowa in the eye seems full enough
to spill across the continent
      if not across the world.

Seeds

Though the meadow's dotted swiss and the mountain's tree-shade finery can be seen by any eye open and ready for a pause, nearly all the other blossoms in God's garden are but ideals and ideas idle for the most part in the mind of humanity. Yet His garden blooms without respect to season or the little tilling and turning of the soil we give it. Imagine what a welcome hired hand each of us would be at harvest or planting time.

I'd Like to Try

I'd put roots down if I could sink them deeper than the plow could tear, down into the earth so far that they could not be flushed by floods or fed by any but the hardest, longest rain.

To be sure that I had once belonged, I'd grow tentacles so long that giants would look longingly upon my roots and me and my longevity.

I may not get the chance again to help somebody build his life, but if I do, I'd like to try to help make his foundation, and my own pilings too, one and the same and strong.

If we kill a man or woman we kill a bit of ourselves. But a cat, too, is an extension of God.

God never meant for any of us to go through life without hope. We were created to be open to all the possibilities life offers, aware of life's demands, and always awake to the beauty He surrounded us with.

With little raw material but sand, the sea has made two hundred thousand mountains that we'll likely never know.

This being so, is it too much to ask that each of us in our lifetime make a single contribution, both unique and useful, that no one walking down the beach has yet had talent to come up with?

To dream is to remain always open.

I'm Strong but I Like Roses

(from the song)

Once in every lifetime
a little bird may come
alone and forgotten
knocked down by the sun.
Every man may choose
to turn and walk away
or take the bird into his hand
and bid him stay.

A man may like roses
and still be big and strong
and what is life without
a little bird's song?

I'm strong, but I like roses
and if a bird should come
I'll keep him till
his singin's all done.

I'm strong, but I like roses
and if the bird should fly
I'll pick another rose
and let the days
go slowly by.

God in His Wisdom made not only seas
and seasons, ground and growing things,
but time aplenty for each of us to know
and to enjoy his inventions and creations.
Too often we do not go easy through the
day, take our time, settle in awhile to just
enjoy the wonder. Maybe if we did we'd
not only enjoy our lives a little more but
learn to appreciate this, His, most unusual
world.

Bend Down and Touch Me
(from the song)

Bend down and touch me
with your eyes
let every morning
hold a sweet surprise
so when I tumble
from my sleep
yours is the first face
that I'll see.

And as I amble
through the day
be there to guide me
all along the way
if I should stumble and I fall
your shoulder's near enough
                    to touch.

Follow me
from darkness into light
then we'll go right back again
through every midnight.

Bend down and touch me
with your eyes
make every evening
hold a new surprise
so when I tumble into sleep
yours is the last face
                    that I'll see.

Pastures Green

(from the song)

Each man must find a pasture green
somewhere beyond the western wind,
out where a man can hear
freedom singin' in his ear,
where love, like lightning, touches him.

Some men were born to live each day
fenced in by pavements cold and gray,
but some men can never wait,
locked outside freedom's gate,
they need to find a pasture green.

Tied by the silver thread of time
love comes to each and every man.
And love, when it comes to you
always seems as fresh and new
as God's own wondrous pastures green.

I know each hill is high and wide
but green pastures fill the other side
and so I'll travel each trail
and ford each stream
and lie down in peace in a pasture
            cool and green.

We are taught that self-control and self-purification are of overriding importance, but our Maker wants us to take chances. No one road or alleyway, even that of abstinence, is the only way or sure way to gain God's favor. He asks that we take risks, that we be outward in our thoughts so that we are able to come to Him with the full knowledge of good and evil. In so doing, we understand all that life affords. Even the shadings between right and wrong should be experienced. Only knowing the full spectrum of life allows us free roads, affords us conscience, takes us straight to God, and makes us better servants and more useful acolytes. Knowing that we've missed nothing, we reach the realm of reason by trying everything. As Christians we come at last upon the true and lasting way. It pleases God that we undertake adventure. It pleases Him even more when we are finally, through trial and error, able to truly distinguish between right and wrong.

From *The City*

A city ought to be cathedral-like
a monument man made
a tool to his betterment
consecrated after due deliberation
to what he believes to be his God.
Whatever that god is
be He supernatural or scientific,
a specific thing
or a trumped-up phrase
that has a different ring
for every man.

We owe it to ourselves
if not some God somewhere
to try to make our cities match
His mountains, His oceans, and His mountain streams.

Never let some teacher tell you
that a city is inanimate.
A city is nothing more than people.
Different colors, different kinds
a hundred different thoughts
inside each head
and since God—whatever, whoever that is—
made each of us a little different
or so we'd like to seem
inside each head
inhabiting the city
lurks a different dream.

Good farmers don't harass the ground—
until the ground is ready.

Thunder is the father of the rain.

Fields of Wonder are the places God goes walking in.

To know a tree and watch it change through its own seasons is to be on speaking terms with God.

The surest way to God is down the same highway Christians have worn into a footpath through the centuries. It is not without its rocks and pitfalls, but once started the end is always clear and straight ahead.

The Wind of Change

(from the song)

Quietly
like the breeze
that blows the olive tree
the wind of change
has come down
from the hills
to lead me home again
through the last mile of sunshine.

As easily
as the moon makes patterns
on the lifeless lake
man grinds the flowers
of the fields beneath his heels
and you wonder if he feels
love, or even boredom,
and my friend —
the wind of change
is asking questions.

Suddenly
there are now
so many giants everywhere
so many men who think
even God looks small
when they're walking tall
and the wind of change is troubled.

Could it be
that He smiles because
He's seen this all before
and He knows the world
is finally going back to dust
and if we trust those men
who trample on the grass
emptiness is all that we
can hope to ask for.

Listen and hear
the sound of
the dying grass bleed
it's bleeding for man
and the poor fool
just won't understand
and it's too late to change
the wind of change.

A Prayer of Consummation

Dear God, I thank you—we thank you—for the gift of life and for the chance to give life. We pray for the father's love, the mother's health and well-being, and for our children a world where each can grow in harmony with all else that You have made.

A Prayer of Privilege

Lord of the universe, we thank You for the world we live in and for the sensibility You have provided us with. We pray that You will help to keep us from taking for granted the privileges You so freely give us.

BROTHERHOOD

There are no wise men or women, only people who go on gaining wisdom by staying alert and being open. By demonstrating their concern for one another, by showing it. Brotherhood is only love by yet another name.

Brotherhood and Family

Most of us are anxious to improve our circumstances—the place where we live, the jobs we hold, our friendships, and our financial situations. How often we forget to take the first step: to improve ourselves. The man or woman who shrinks from self-examination can never hope to accomplish the many things he or she feels a need for. This is as true of earthly matters as of heavenly matters. The body is the servant of the mind, and it is important that both master and servant constantly remain healthy. Just as people who live in fear of a disease are the people who get it, those who take simple measures to keep their minds and bodies clean will find they seldom need repair. A simple but meaningful meditation: *If you would perfect your body, guard your mind. If you would renew your body, beautify your mind.*

The mind is the dwelling place of hatred and bigotry. If we are to be of service to ourselves and to God, we must be ever mindful that we are not alone in this world or in our neighborhood. Because our neighbor may have different ideas and ideologies than we do, a different religion and different rules to live by, or was created in a different hue, does not in any way make that person better or worse than we are. That is a fact of life, as large a reality as you will find in your lifetime and probably the most important single truth you should commit to memory. As bigots or as people who fail to take into account other people's thoughts and needs and ideas, we can never hope to be in God's good grace.

This world is made up of many disenfranchised people, and many more who never had anything to begin with. At this late date in American history, the resistance to women who are demanding equality in life is a poor comment not only on where we've come from but where, as God-loving and God-fearing people, we are going.

It is fact, not fiction, that we may have arrived at a time in our society when we no longer deserve children—those incredible works of God. The story of the battered child, the neglected child, the mentally- or sexually-abused child rarely makes the front pages of the newspapers, because the occurrences are so common. These neglected, directionless, put-upon, and hurt children are everywhere. Some will not live to become adults; others will go from foster home, to truancy, to reform school, to crime, and to prison. One wonders if there will ever be a Bill of Rights for children, a simple set of rules that would guarantee at least the essentials: good schooling, small classrooms, plentiful teachers, and care and love at home, instead of what little there is to be found in the streets.

Some of our brothers and sisters have different affectional preferences than we do—in fact, if we are each of us unique, as we surely are, certainly we cannot expect any two people or two sets of people to be the same—so affection, like a human

51

being's ability at mathematics, is only his or her own business.

The Black man is not a minority. The Oriental and the Chicano are not special to themselves. The Jew is not isolated and out of the mainstream. *Each* of us is a minority. Each minority contributes to the majority. All of us as individuals are set apart by what we do and how we react to other individuals. The dividing lines between us are not nationality, race, color, lack of intellect or super-intellect, or religion. We are told that Christ died for all of us and so even the non-believer deserves a place in this world, a place of his or her own choosing. We cannot go to heaven as a Baptist who doesn't believe in brotherhood, or a Methodist uninterested in mankind. Being Jewish does not guarantee us a safe crossing over the River Jordan and into the arms of God, unless we believe in justice as well as Judea. What is required is that we all see every person as a unique and equal fellow human being. Each of us has to go beyond the narrow boundaries within which we choose to imprison ourselves.

Until all women and men are sisters and brothers, the gates to heaven will continue to need periodic oiling and protection against rust.

Do not be quick to judge people by their outward appearance or what you may feel are unorthodox ways. There was a man once, long ago, who walked and never ran, lived in a cave, wore his hair long, and never shaved. He even went about the countryside dressed in a flowing robe speaking against the government under which he lived, condemning the rich, and always siding with the poor. He was alone most of the time, but many of his friends were thieves, cripples, children, and people who had been abandoned by society. His name was Jesus.

Each time we show another human being kindness or charity without any thought of gain for ourselves, we become—if not the right arm of our savior—some small extension of God.

The Holy Spirit is attracted to the sinner first, since challenge is His business. But to retain His full attention we must improve our habits and go forward.

Only when we stop whining and begin to joust with ill will and injustice does God bring out His ladder, propping it against the wall to make it easier for us to reach the other side.

Our own sense of injury and persecution is left behind when we begin to dwell upon the problems of the other men and women who live with us on this earth.

We should have fewer friends than we have time for so that we can give each one extra time.

To turn away from friendship offered
is to turn your back on part of life.

Small boys need encouragement; the freight trains in their minds will only take them just so far. Be kind, for small boys need to grow.

Jesus met the woman at the well and was kind to her. He didn't ask if she had sinned or gone against life's principles—she poured out her thoughts and worries and a feeling of shame to Him. He listened. If *we* took more time to listen, pontificated and judged less, we could be of greater service to God's family.

I measure success by how well I sleep on a given night. If I have not had to question my motives for any particular action I might have undertaken, or knowingly caused another human being trouble or discomfort, then I am at peace with my God and myself and I fall asleep easily.

If sleep comes hard, then I know the day has been a personal failure.

The Summer's Long

(from the song)

A friend lay dying
and I could have said,
raise your head a little
and I'll try to show you Spain.
But he slipped away
and I'll never have the chance again.
And the summer's long, long, long,
and the summer's long.

There was a man so hungry
and I could have given bread,
bread costs very little
it's much cheaper than the rain.
But he went away
and I'll never have the chance again.
And the summer's long, long, long,
and the summer's long.

There was a girl who loved me
and I could have held her head
against my chest
and helped to ease her pain.
But she's gone away
and I'll never have the chance again.
And the summer's long, long, long,
and the summer's long.

There is a world so needy
but we treat it like it's dead,
I don't know what
we all expect to gain.
One day it will be gone
and we'll never have the chance again.
And the summer's long, long, long,
and the summer's long.

The arrogant love to tell us—even threaten—that there is only one sure way to heaven. Theirs. That is not so. A thousand roads there are, just as there are trees that wrap the world around with different kinds of fruit.

We are made or unmade by ourselves; we forge the weapons in our own armory of thought, and we make the tools to build for ourselves fortresses of strength and joy and peace. By the right application of thought, we ascend to divine perfection. It is also within our power to abuse our powers of thought and descend below the level of the lowest beast.

Because a woman or man sits quietly, not speaking—even staring straight ahead or looking down—do not presume that person is lonely or without friends. We meditate in different ways.

No one likes to be locked up or imprisoned. None of us is happy in a cell, be it one of our own making or one constructed for us by an enemy. But it is useless to continuously mistrust people, letting ill-will, cynicism, or non-constructive thoughts clutter up our thinking, Suspicion and envy can be a cell without a padlock. Turning the other cheek is not only less difficult than most of us suspect it to be, but it is one of the easiest ways to feel good about ourselves.

It is not enough to call a man your brother, or a woman your sister. You must *believe* that it is so.

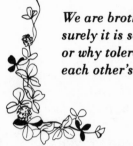

We are brothers and sisters,
surely it is so
or why tolerate
each other's mischief?

Resolution I

Out of the sad mistaken belief that as a man I must behave as all men do, I've turned my back a time too often. God, help me keep a resolution that I make today: Not to walk head high past someone I can help.

Resolution II

Hold me accountable, O God, for my failures. Help me turn each sorrow I have unthinkingly caused someone else into an intended joy.

Keep me safe from my own ignorance. When I lie, let me speak the falsehood aloud that I may not repeat the same transgression.

I'll Catch the Sun

(from the song)

I'll catch the sun
and never give it back again.
I'll catch the sun
and keep it for my own.
And in a world where no one understands
I'll take my outstretched hand
and offer it to anyone
who comes along and tells me
he's in need of love.
In need of hope or maybe just a friend.
Perhaps in time I'll even share my sun
with that new anyone
to whom I gave my hand.

God saves the poor from their oppressors,
and the oppressors from themselves.

Freedom is taken for granted except by those who feel oppressed. If you have conquered weakness and put away all selfish thoughts, thereby making yourself open to receive God, you belong neither to the oppressor nor are you oppressed. You are free.

Love is a feeling not easily taught . . . but each of us should attempt to be each other's pupil as well as teacher.

It's not merely that women are as good as men, or better. Each of us is son or daughter of the Lord Almighty and nothing more than that—only His children. Knowing this, how can we be anything but equal.

Those who travel gentle in the world are seldom recognized as gentlemen by others. It matters not, for gentleness toward another human being is the thin line between success and failure for each of us.

No one can lead a blind man into church and hope for his salvation. He must walk into the house of God himself.

To live only for the sunlight is to deny yourself the shadings shadows bring.

Women prime the pumps, but how often do they get their share of water?

God seldom grades us on how well or ill we do, but we should always be willing to grade ourselves. Charity, and knowing our own capabilities better than we do those of others, should keep us from determining another human being's failure or success.

We are chained only by ourselves. Thought and action are the jailers of bigotry and indolence just as they are the liberating angels that free us to be ourselves. We do not receive what we wish and pray for— only what we justly earn. Our prayers are only answered when they are in harmony with God's own expectations of ourselves and our environment.

If brotherhood becomes a burden, you must keep reexamining yourself. Doing something for another human being should never be anything less than an act of joy.

Those people who believe a woman to be a second-class citizen, or a person of a different religion, culture, sexual orientation, or color to be not quite as good as they are, are second-class themselves, suffering from arrested mental and spiritual development.

God not only expects us to get along together, but to get on with it—living, loving one another, and moving toward His good grace.

Equality means not only equal rights, but equal responsibility to one's neighbor and one's self.

A Prayer for Myself

I have stumbled and fallen somewhere in this day. Raise me up again, my Lord, that I might work for You, and in so doing work for my own salvation, and the salvation of my brothers and sisters. If I have lied, enlarged on truth, or made up fact, instruct me, Lord, in the true way.

If I have sinned against my neighbor, I have no excuse. If I have coveted what is my neighbor's, I have no excuse. If I have been distant to a friend or stranger, I have no alibi that will justify my actions, and if I think I have, teach me otherwise.

Take me from myself and let me serve You while I breathe Your air. Let me worship You. Let me share Your kindness with those men and women of God I know and will come to know.

A Prayer for Our Special Brothers and Sisters

To those who cannot pray. To those who cannot walk upon your ground. To those who cannot see the world around them. To those who cannot speak. To those in misery or discomfort. To those poor of means or poor of spirit. To those who feel oppressed or put upon. To those who have not found You yet. Oh, Lord, for these our sisters and brothers known and not known to us, we ask that You take special care and note their special problems. We ask that You provide the wisdom for all of us to care for each other and help each other.

THE NECESSITY OF LOVE

We may only be *two*, but that makes us stronger than *one* and, with God's help, gives us the capability of armadas.

Love

Over the years, in attempting to define or re-
define love, I've filled whole books. I've said that
"love, at best, is giving what you need to get," that
it is "tied about the throats of cats, now near, now
sounding far away," and "that it doesn't matter
who you love or how you love, but *that* you love."
But *I love, therefore I am* is too simple. We may be
lifted on high by love, but to stay there we must
continue to care for what we left below, remember-
ing that it is not only possible but necessary to
share our newfound love.

It may be that we have used the word "love" so
much that its meaning has become obscured. The
dictionary tells us that love is (1) the profoundly
tender or passionate affection for a person of the
opposite sex; (2) a feeling of warm personal attach-
ment or deep affection, as for a parent, child, or
friend; (3) a person toward whom love is felt; be-
loved person; sweetheart; (4) affectionate concern
for the well-being of others; (5) strong predilec-
tion or liking for anything; (6) the object or thing
so liked; and, finally, (7) the benevolent affection
of God for His creatures, or the reverent affection
due God from them. Despite the dictionary's many
definitions, love is both more and less than the

descriptions of those who do our thinking for us.

The supply of love will never exceed the demand, but it should. Love is an attitude, and one from which we should not stray far in our actions toward ourselves and toward others. The word "peace" is so often coupled with "love" that sometimes the two words seem synonymous. Love is tranquility. But it can also be the height of excitement, or, when one feels unloved, the depth of depression. Most of all, love is another word for sharing. If you go out into the day and beyond the day with love in mind, then you are probably as close to God as you can ever hope to be.

To love, you need not even be two. Alone, you can love and love honestly; but if you expect a return on your investment, the surest way to guarantee it is to love your God, Who will teach you to love yourself. Only then will you be capable of loving yet another. The woman or the man who complains that she or he, while loving, gave everything and received nothing in return, has not stepped through love's doorway. It is not possible to love someone or something fully and not to be in receipt of more than you have given.

Few of us are ready to love anyone else—even God—until we learn to know and love ourselves. That isn't easy, and it shouldn't be. It is difficult both to love that much, and—seemingly—that little.

Together we are a community. God is not so much the head of that community as He is a part of us. The mystery of creation is the mystery of God. The reality we know as love is God's reality. Each of us has known love on many levels: romantic love, the love of good friends, the love of family, of nature, of a particular kind of work, and the love of God. As complex as these many kinds of love are, we understand them. If we truly love nature and all of God's creation, we should accept them as symbols of faith. Then the faith that is as inexplicable as love ought to be at once explainable.

Creed

*It doesn't matter
who you love
or how you love
but that you love.*

*For in the end
the act of loving anyone
is the act of loving God.*

If God could give His son for love, we can offer up our smiles.

You are the end of me, and my new beginning.

Love should be as endless as a life without illness, a tree that grows within a climate of perfection during its young years so that it becomes stronger against the onslaught of the elements, a season of sunlight with only morning clouds for contrast.

By leaning on someone you love,
you help to hold him up.

I'm in a hurry; I have no time to hate. But I have all the hours in the days still left to me to give to love.

God's handiwork is as fleeting as a passing thought and as solid as a stone.

Sunday is for singing quiet songs and for loving everything you come in contact with.

With God in our hearts and love in our arms we needn't be afraid of poverty or blindness.

Walk down the day easy, knowing your security is going where you go—together.

The faces of children are proof enough of God.

Boundaries

I love you enough
to let you run
but far too much
to let you fly.
I'll let you walk
the block's end
      by yourself
sail off on any lake
    or silent sea
but if I peer at you
as you go wandering
through noisy rooms
know that I keep watch
for both of us.
I love you enough
to let you run
but far too much
to let you fly.

Whatever litany of love you use is up to you, but let it be the testament of touch to keep the cold out.

You love me with your patience.
How hard you work and how hard you try.

It is not possible to be in love
and be very far away from God.

God meant no one to live without loving
and being loved.

Two against a winter morning are sure to claim one more victory over chance and trouble.

To love it is more important to learn the needs of others than to always be aware of your own needs.

Love—being the right hand of God— should be given with compassion.

Love is imitating Christ enough to let Him know it . . . even when it isn't Sunday.

Hold on to love . . . or it might let you go. Take not your faith for granted; it must be practiced to remain worthwhile. So, too, with love. In loving someone, you cannot admit it often enough.

No one can measure on a scale what love is worth
. . . though one small gesture sometimes tallies the
amount as sure as any seasoned teller could.

I celebrate the God who gave me you.

God asks only that we be as open with our love
as we are with our desire for living. He respects the
time we need within the shadows just as He knows
any love, in order to be worthwhile, must stand the
test of sunlight.

None of us is so wealthy or influential that we cannot be further enriched by love.

A present of reality is made by truth
as much as it is shaped by love.

I've seen those who drove into love without a learner's permit. The result was usually an accident.

Love cannot be said aloud too often
or spoken in silence too many times.

The Lovers of December

(from the song)

White winter knows no age
it's like the printed word
that dances on the page
and so they go still smiling
though their heads bend low,
a smile as golden as September
the lovers of December.

Gray morning knows no day
and when you touch it
it's quick to run away
and so they turn to watch
the fire of Autumn burn
until the flames are but an ember
the lovers of December.

There's a time to love
and a time to cry
time to catch the bird
time to let it fly.
Time to hear the chariot coming
and step aside
for the road is as narrow
as the heart is wide.

Black midnight knows no year
it's hard to see, just like
the color of a tear.
And now they pause,
unraveling what wasn't and what was,
a ribbon of remember
the lovers of December.

There's a time when God
looks you in the eye
lets you trade your life
for a piece of sky.
Time to hear the trumpets sounding
and move ahead,
when the Leader beckons
let yourself be led.

Soft sunsets seem to say
the smile of God is just
a breath or two away,
and now they stop, as easily
as any spinning top
for life is tentative but tender
the lovers of December

Give me your strongest smile
and in return
I'll let you have my hand.
These are presents quite enough
for two who love each other
*   and each other's God.*

A Prayer of Joy

Dear God, share our joy. We are happy with each other. We want You to know how much You've helped us, and we pray You will continue to be there not only when we are apart or at odds with one another, but during times, like this, when we are happy with one another, the world around us, and, most importantly, joyous because our God is the light of our union. You guide and guard the life we attempt to build, and with your help we will stay together and grow together.

A NEW MARRIAGE CEREMONY

Loving and the act of love is only one
more affirmation that God in heaven walks
and runs and somersaults—living to see
all things His hands created die, rise, and
live again.

Coming Together in the
Presence of God

There is certainly a convincing argument for staying single. Some people seem happy alone, others unwilling to make the intense commitment, concentration, and letting go of ego that both parties must bring to marriage.

I believe in marriage. It is sensible, important if two people want children, and a necessary part of Christian belief and culture. Further, there are ample references in the Scriptures not only to the desirability of marriage, but Christ's own belief that matrimony is an essential part of a complete life—especially one involving two people who love each other and who desire to work and live together.

There is, or should be, something basically honest in a union sanctified by God—whether in His church or on a mountain top. I have never been a moralist, full of instructions and set ideas, ready to preach to anyone who'll listen. But certain beliefs and ideologies are hard to shake off.

The clergy and the courts most often use the excuse that matrimony binds two people and keeps them bound, lessening the chance of divorce because papers and an actual contract are involved. To me this is the least and probably the poorest excuse for two people who love each other to legalize their union. My reasoning is simple:

(1) Too many couples stay together out of habit, or because of the stigma that divorce still brings in some quarters. A bad habit is a bad habit, whether it involves drinking, smoking, carelessness behind the steering wheel, spending more than one can afford, ill feelings toward a neighbor, or a marriage that has lost the spark that ignited and created it in the first place.

(2) How often have you heard someone say "we" or "they" are only living together for the sake of the children?

That argument assumes that the parties being discussed have long ago lost respect and love for each other. An unhappy home has seldom produced a happy, healthy child. Though children need and should have guidance and love from both mother and father, one good parent is always preferable to two unhappy individuals attempting to divide their parental obligations—and certainly preferable to no parent at all.

(3) Though the clergy would just as soon not speak about it, much of our organized religion has not kept up with the times and the changing needs of people—particularly in regard to marriage and the family. If marriage vows are to be used at all, they need updating. Last year, more than half the couples in the United States and one-third of those in Great Britain who fell in love or sought the companionship of another, elected to live together without benefit of wedlock.

So much has happened and so many changes have occurred in our lifestyle since "love, honor, and obey" (love, honor—yes; but I wouldn't ask a dog to give me blind obedience) was instituted. No one should be another's servant. Whether we are talking about wife or husband—each human being was created by God and therefore is entitled to equality, respect, and an equal share of the joy that a good marriage brings.

"Till death do us part" is unrealistic. Of course, every relationship should be entered into with the hope that it will last a lifetime, and couples should be cognizant of the work it takes to make any relationship strong and lasting. But to expect two people to remain together after they've discovered their union does not and cannot work, is wrong even in God's eyes. He wants us to be useful in this world He's made—to ourselves and to the family of humanity. What parents do not have that desire for their children?

Yes, lifelong fidelity is devoutly to be wished by the couple involved, and certainly it is a rule set down and sent down by God Himself. I somehow feel that He meant it more as a prayer than a rule. Once the joy, respect, understanding, and love that only two people can bring to each other has been lost, forgotten, or ignored—counseling, straight talk, and hard work should be attempted by both parties to make a marriage stick and grow. But if the marriage fails to take seed or dies completely, the problem should be discussed intelligently and compassionately. Then, if dissolution is the only answer, the union should be ended, thus allowing two people to be useful and productive again for others.

Though my marriage ceremony has been sent on request to more than five thousand couples, with at least three thousand that we know of using it, I primarily see it as a suggestion to those who prefer their own vows.

I would caution anyone taking vows to include God in the words they and their pastor speak. A union made in the eyes of the Father has more chance of growing into permanency than something done behind His back. It should be obvious that the greatest force for good on earth or in heaven is a definite plus in our lives. And don't be afraid, through the years, to talk with God and ask His advice on your togetherness.

The Rod McKuen
Marriage Ceremony

Pastor:
In the presence of God, the hosts, those beings we believe in but cannot always see, I pronounce these names:

_____ and

_____ .

We come together in this clearing to join hands and in so doing, to make a pair of souls into a third, for the glory of God, for the good of our fellow human beings, for the needs of these two people. When we walk away, these persons will be as they were when they came, equal in every way yet different because they will be equal parts of each other.

Couple (unison):
We desire to stay together, work together under the fatherhood of our God.

Pastor:
That is as it should be.

Couple (unison):
We desire to be together as long as we can bring each other love, friendship, companionship and help.

Pastor:
That is as it should be.

Person on right to person on left:
My mind is clean, my body is clean, and I offer them to you before God and before my friends assembled here.

Person on left to person on right:
My mind is clean, my body is clean, and I offer them to you before God and before my friends assembled here.

Pastor:
That is as it should be, and in the time to come you will bring each other love as yet not known to you both and that knowledge of yourselves that you do not yet know. This is a marriage, not a contract. This is a union with no set of rules but those you set upon yourselves. God gave His children minds so that they might think. God gave you, His children, consciences, so that you will always think with temperance. Only through mutual respect and love will this union live and thrive.

Couple (unison):
We have come together to stay together.

Pastor:
It will be so as long as you want it to be so, and if you should stop wanting or caring then you should part. Not as a thief going in the night. Not in anger or in harshness but with sensibility and respect. God did not mean for us to live alone, nor did He wish us to live together without caring and without respect.

Couple (unison):
We have a need for one the other.

Pastor, to person on right:
This is the Holy Sacrament done in the presence of God. For me to join two lives together you must believe that your need is genuine and transcends all.

Person on right:
I believe that to be so.

Pastor, to person on left:
This is the Holy Sacrament done in the presence of God. For me to join two lives together you must believe that your need is genuine and transcends all.

Person on left:
I believe that to be so.

Pastor:
This is a covenant with the Almighty—whatever you believe the Almighty to be.

Couple (unison):
We believe that by leaning on each other we will hold each other up.

Pastor:
This is a vow for forever. If forever should end for the two of you, or one of you tomorrow, or next year, stay together only as long as you need each other. Go only when your need for the other ends.

Person on right:
I believe in love. I believe the person I will walk away with today to start another lifetime with to be someone I wish to comfort and I will expect comfort in return. I will share whatever I have to share, and I will always expect the sharing and the loving to be returned.

Pastor:
It is good that people come together.

Person on left:
I believe in the power of love. The power of goodness. I assert, and I believe, that coming together with this person broadens my own capacity for love. I will respect my love, not because I am told to but because it is my desire to share all that I have with this chosen one. I will work as we have pledged to work together, for ourselves, and more, for each other.

Pastor:
It is good. You are part of the family of man and at one with that spirit about and around us.

Couple (unison):
Bless us. Pray for us and sanction our union. Help us to remember that we are separate but we are equal.

Pastor:
I bless you. The Holy Spirit blesses you. What you believe to be God blesses you and believes you.

Person on left to person on right:
I trust you. You honor me by letting me begin with you this new life. I give my life to you, in God's name.

Person on right to person on left:
I give my life to you in God's name because I trust you, because you honor me by letting me begin with you this new life.

**Best Man, Lady in Waiting or Friend
(holder of the rings or garlands):**
These rings, these garlands are but a symbol.

Couple (unison):
A symbol of a perfect day and the start of a perfect life.

Pastor:
God of the heavens, Lord of the universe, divine being who makes all things—whoever you are, wherever you are—join with me and bless this union. Let them rise to those heights only love can guarantee and assure.

Couple (unison):
We love and we desire to be together for today and for always.

Pastor:
From this hour onward you are together. You are together for all of us here who see you and those not present.

Couple (unison):
Bless us, please.

Pastor:
You are blessed because you have each other. You are married for as long as each of you wish togetherness.

Couple:
(Present rings, or necklaces, or flowers, or join hands.)

Pastor:
Each human being is in God's eye equal. Before you were two, now you are one, more, you are three, because being one your love has given birth and increased your capacity in every way. I pray that you will stay together for forever. It is my desire that forever lasts until the final, not always just, hand of death separates you, and that you will be joined again in the world beyond. I love you as you love each other and yourselves. I say that you are joined, that you are married.

Those gathered:
Amen.

Couple:
Kiss.

A Marriage Prayer

Almighty God, sanction our marriage and our family. Help each of us never to do anything to debase or cause ill-feeling in those we love. Bring us closer together and closer to You, that we might, by caring for each other, serve You in the best way we know how for all our days to come.

A Prayer to the Protector

God protect our sometimes troubled union. Encourage us to encourage each other to turn to You in time of trouble or distress.

ON LONELINESS AND BEING ALONE

Never fear being alone, because you never are.

Loneliness

One is usually not lonely for Schenectady or Paris or humanity, but for *someone*. He or she has left us, died, or is missing, and has thus betrayed us.

Loneliness is often self-induced, and being lonely could be considered selfish. Since the cure for selfishness is being willing to share, the remedy for certain kinds of loneliness is seeking out others, befriending them, or even asking their help.

Don't fear asking for aid if you are troubled or alone. The time for real concern is when you find yourself afraid to risk the company of others.

We are a nation—a world—of travelers, not content to be in one place long. Friendships suffer with each move, each change of residence or location. There is no time to build a storehouse of warmth and friendship that will nourish us and keep us from being lonely. Even love of our work or vocation can give way to feelings of depression when we are shunted from one city to another, moved to a different part of a building, or even moved to another area of work in the same department.

As modern society becomes more complex, our friendships tend to be shallow ones. We become unwilling to learn more about our friends' lives, or to dig beneath the surface of what they offer us without our asking. A friendship is a give-and-take business, yet as individuals we seldom open up when questioned or challenged. In this age, existing friendships suffer, too. Old ties are forgotten and new attempts at making friends can be like crossing a battleground while the enemy fire still rages— especially when we know these new acquaintances will undoubtedly remain just that—acquaintances. Jealousy, possessiveness, and feeling that we lack support all contribute to our loneliness. The more attention we give the seed of loneliness, the more we allow it to grow.

As a society, we have carefully created a leisure class that enjoys shorter working hours and more fringe benefits. But, instead of husbanding its precious free time, this same leisure class gives it over to the technician and the inventor who build bigger and better—and more impersonal—services. There are more television sets in our homes than there are telephones. We see TV personalities more often than we speak to our friends. And now, with video games, recorders, and satellites to bring dozens of new channels into our homes, the TV screen has become not only a form of entertainment but a babysitter, a conversationalist, and our chief means of keeping in touch with the world around us. We are in imminent danger of thinking of television as one of our best friends.

In the sixties, I wrote a poem entitled "The Days of the Dancing," in which I lamented that socially we were dancing six feet apart and often to mirrors. Two decades later, popular dancing still affords us the opportunity for movement without touching. Radio talk shows around the clock emit disembodied voices we can call on the telephone. These voices sometimes listen to our problems, frustrations, and anxieties—until they become bored or don't know the answer to a question, and then, with a click, cut off our monologue in mid-sentence. Thus, we are offered a new form of alienation and aloneness. Perhaps we need to go fishing or to a ball game, for a drive, a healthy walk, a visit to the theater—anything that will get us out of the house—and out of ourselves. A change of scenery is one of the most effective cures for feeling lost and lonely.

Many people confuse being alone with loneliness. It is true that each may lead to the other, but each is a distinctive state. Being lonely is often a painful experience, but being alone can be very valuable. A certain amount of time by ourselves or in the company of God clears our brain and helps to regiment and reorganize our lives. Without some "think time," we relinquish our quest for knowledge to others and are forced to accept their opinions as our own.

Our character—or lack of it—becomes the product of what we hear or read or see on television, and not what we find out by digging into our own hearts and minds and subconscious. There should always be time for meditating, thinking, and praying. We need God not just for prayer and meditation, but to talk to in a way we can't talk with anyone else.

Abandoned by love, the lover pines. The widow, whose partner suddenly dies, feels not only abandonment but the sense that she has nowhere to go. The child who interrupts the six o'clock news with what is to him or her an important question—only to be told to go out and play—stops questioning. The elderly parent is shunted off to a retirement village, a leisure world, or a community that consists only of people of similar age. We sons and daughters, by putting our parents in such concentration camps, are taking from them their self-respect. At the very time when their understanding of themselves and the world about them is at its peak, they are told, in effect, that they are no longer of use to anyone. A life of shuffleboard and needlepoint is hardly a proper reward for years of service to a community, to a job, and, most of all, to family and friends.

We are now in the grip of a new, all-pervasive urge to own "things." These things are no longer limited to automobiles, houses, fine linen, etc.— "things" now include those we take as mates. We strive to manage, manipulate, and dominate the so-called beloved for our own individual pleasure. A love that dominates is not love but the most ill-gotten and ill-used form of possessiveness. True love is totally open and committed to sharing not just the good times and the great moments together or apart, but the frustrations, loneliness, despair, and hurt as well.

Loneliness is like guerrilla warfare. It undermines the individual, the community, and the country. God did not mean for us to be lonely or He would not have created other human beings, the plant life that makes our world so beautiful, and the animals both domestic and wild that give us so much pleasure. If you are lonely go to God. There is certainly Someone with whom you can attempt a dialogue. When it comes to being lonely, psychiatry is a plaything. Too much self-criticism is destructive, but an open smile directed toward another individual is a passport to getting better. Don't take what I say on faith. Try it.

101

A Lesson

If God walked on the earth disguised as Christ today, He would be considered a loner. But in imitating Christ we mustn't once forget He seldom went alone. His friends were those who needed friends themselves.

A teacher, He was often taught, and not by just His Father but by the flock He shepherded from torment into love.

He was the wisest of His wise men. That didn't come by chance; it came from caring.

Only the lonely are free from convention
but only the lonely are bound by themselves.

I'm not afraid of what's upcoming or what has
gone before, and if there's nothing left to know
about or learn, I'll review the early lessons yet
again.

Sometimes we use whole paragraphs to say what
silence might better express. The same is not true
for prayer. The longer our dialogues with God and
the more frequently we attempt them, the greater
our chance of coming upon truths we can genuinely
call our own. Discoveries unique to us.

If God could give His son for love and God—and
so that we might never be alone—the least we can
do is offer up our smiles.

Not Always Alone

There are people in the world who quietly go their own way, secure within themselves that what they do is honest. Never must the world be judge or jury. The payment rests with God, the verdict known to those men and women only and carried in their private pockets.

If we must judge, let us first use the mirror on our own wall for practice.

Perspective has its problems, but all we need do is look into a stranger's or a friend's good eyes to see the sunset's truest color. Better than a crystal ball or the most advanced kaleidoscope.

The mind, even more than the spirit, is the dwelling place of loneliness. If we think we are lonely, loneliness can almost always be induced.

Those who are dead to dreaming live within a cloud of their own making, and so their chance of entering the stratosphere is scant.

I close my eyes to dreaming
only long enough to dream.

Dreams run to reality, and once or twice the marriage works; though in the end reality dissolves completely into dream.

Before befriending butterflies
you have to meet with midnight moths.

The Singer and the Song

Jesus, can you hear me singing?
Is my voice tuned loud enough?
Am I mixing with the choir
or soloing an edge out front?

Jesus, at the echo's ending
is my song still strong and true
or has it blended with the mudlark
and been lost in silver forests?

Jesus, is an answer coming
to the prayers I prayed before
or should I repeat them now
and settle down to wait again?

Jesus, pardon me for asking
but will you grant me one more hour
to your own or to my liking
so that I might work with you?

Sunrise

How is it sunrise strikes a different chord each day? Soft one morning, loud and full of life and self-importance on the next. I have ridden off to work with sunrises I remember to this day, and sat upon the sand greeting summer sun on Sundays when I had nothing else to do, no one else to sit and talk and sing to. God, make the sunrise come today, but softly, for I'm alone. You needn't shout, for there'll be no one else but me to hear.

DEATH AS
A BEGINNING

Death is not our final hour, we have God's
promise on that.

On Leaving

Death finally comes. No vain image in a mirror, declining to recognize its true age (in a mirror we see what we want to see), can stop the process of aging. It is important to understand that death is logical and preordained. From our birth we begin moving toward death. It may be that death upon this earth is only the shrugging off of a body grown weary, so that the soul can display itself in some better place.

To be a Christian is to believe that death is a prelude to another life. However, it is not necessary to believe in God to feel that perhaps something better lies ahead. We know little of the so-called afterlife, since no explorer has returned to tell us of the good or bad awaiting us.

Do not be afraid of death. On the other hand, do not dwell on it or attempt to welcome it ahead of time. Although I believe God forgives the taking of our lives in this very complicated world, suicide is not a practical alternative, because tomorrow always carries in its very mystery a promise as well as a threat. And the promise should not be denied.

The Green

I'll survive, I will.
Whatever hill I'm asked
to climb or crawl upon
whatever dry space
I must travel through
to where the green
of this oncoming season
stays to speak to me,
I'll be there.

Wait for me
whoever you are
Whatever tunic or bright shirt
                    you wear,
I'm coming, I'll be there.

The Long Run

Once I thought I'd die at fifty. I had no reason for thinking so, merely that I would have spent the hours allotted to me and it would be time for me to move through the distance to whatever waits when we are separated from life. Now I know that I will not go easy. I enjoy too much the sparring, the skirmishes, and the long runs that only life affords.

Song from the Earth

One drop of rain
cannot fill a fountain.
One grain of sand
cannot make a mountain.
And a handful of earth
is more than we should be worth
in the eyes of the Man
who made us all from the earth.

Those who go alone
those who go together
those who give the world its trouble
those who make it better,
we're all on our way to dust
from the day of our birth,
from the ground we've come
and we're all going back to earth.
So stay for a while with me
walk another mile with me,
live another day for what it's worth.
Tomorrow and tomorrow and tomorrow
we're all going back to the earth.

Phase Three

I think I'm managing
the turn quite well
I'm almost sure of it
I even find myself
greedy for the coming day.

To Begin with...

To begin with, every page is blank, until a word, a smudge, a paragraph is set down upon it. Some pages still stay blank even after the most intricate, indelible story has been started.

The starting of a new story is always easy; it's the ending that comes hard. Knowing when to draw conclusions, a point to let your characters stop leading you so that you can take command. When is the sum enough to provide the summing up?

I do not know how death will come to me, though once I thought I did. How I will greet it will depend on how hard or easy it comes in. I am sure any pain that might accompany my going could not be as bad or worse than some I've known in my life. I am resolved that, if I can, I will view the end as the writer does the blank page just in front of him, a beginning.

Resolution III

*Now comes another year
another chance to say*
Thank you *to old friends
            for hanging in
no matter what the crowd
or circumstances shouted out
or tried to dictate.*

*Private lists
and public resolutions
are part of what
each New Year brings.
So I resolve, both publicly
and in a private way
to try and be a better friend
to those I love
and give more of myself
to those I'll come to care about
in the year just starting.*

*Most of all I'll try
to never once forget,
God is the maker of each thing
that lives or moves or breathes
and so deserves compassion,
indulgence and attention
and at the very least
some measure of our love.*

Earth

Alive, awake
we anguish for the dead
we wail and weep.
But it is for ourselves
              that tears
and tearing at the heart
                  is done.

We do not grieve
because the earth
reclaims its own.
We weep because
we're suddenly deprived
of good companions
      sound judgment
and familiar counsel.

Prayer Before Sleep

Lord, let me live another night, another hour, another minute, that I might try to make up for transgressions, known and unknown, which I have brought about within the day just past. Forgive me, Lord, and help protect me from myself. Help me. For, with Your help, sleep—even that final one—will come easy.

Prayer at Morning

Good morning, God, and thank you for another restful night. Help me achieve these goals I've set for this new day, so that I will have justified this extra time on Earth.

CHRISTMAS EVERY DAY

Christmas is more like Spring than Winter;
and because the name itself means mass
for Christ, there isn't any reason this
holiday or holy day should not be celebrated
all year long.

Celebrating Christ

What follows are poems, songs, and prayers I've written through the years as part of celebrating Christmas. Some were sent as private cards, some are now sung by choirs, a few have even found their way into the pulpit. Others are new, written especially for this book.

For Christians, celebrating the Christ Child's birthday should mean more than midnight services and exchanging gifts. It ought to be a kind of spring, a rededication to God and the Son He sent to earth to save us.

Christmas is a time of celebration. Bright packages and ropes of pine, starched red bows and ribbons, eggnog and plum pudding, all promising we'll be touched by something extraordinary.

But Christmas is a time of memory as much as celebration. For some it is memory of loss, intensified because, for all of our lives, we've seen it as the season of promise. So much promised by friends and family, so little given in the rush. Christmas is and can be lonely. A loneliness that crowds us like no other as we turn inward, farther from reality than at any other season.

Just once we ought to set about preparing for the downhill run that nearly always accompanies the tinsel. The only way to do so is to get outside ourselves and think about the Infant in that manger long ago. Not just remembering His birthday, but remembering the trials and truth that marked His life and, down these many years, also mark ours. We are better because He was the best. Throughout His life He carried the passkeys to His Father's house, then threw them to us from the cross. Whatever went before, life only started when His life began.

God may have been the architect, but He sent Christ, His Son, to be our builder. He showed us in a thousand ways that none of us need ever fear again, that worry is worth nothing, loneliness is self-indulgence, and death is only a passport to everlasting life.

This year, as Christmas makes its round again, resolve to smile inside and out. Carry kindness to its farthest edge, compassion still beyond. And you will finally know yourself. Then, reaching just a little farther through the mists and myths, grasp the outstretched hand of God.

Invitation

I've seen so many Merry Xmas signs
with Christ squeezed out by laziness
or the printer's economic need,
the outrage that it once produced
has almost found its way into the attic
with nineteen-sixty's broken toys.

(Had I not the faces of small children
to mirror Christ for me the whole year long
I might believe God dead, or sleeping anyway.
Though I doubt there lives a Lucifer
who could make September leaves to fall
or set the tails of dogs to wagging.)

God is living somewhere in the mountains,
a recluse from some people's hearts.
But He'd drop by smiling in the chilly night
and help us celebrate His first son's birthday
if we cared enough to leave the porch light on.

Simple Gifts

(from the song)

Though the gift be small and simple
if the wish is wide,
just the simple gift of giving
makes you warm inside.

Though the thought is ever-fleeting
if a thought at all,
remember all the mighty big things
started out as small.

So if you've a gift worth giving
let it be your smile.
Let it be a kindly word
that makes the stranger stop awhile.

Let it be a simple gift then
if the wish is wide,
just the simple gift of giving
makes you warm inside.

Caroling

Christmas
is the celebration
of a Mass for Christ,
the giving of our voices
to the songs of joy
that men have made
to christen that first Christian.
If we relegate that day to Claus—
however glad his entourage,
however bright his gifts may be—
then Jingle Bells should be
our only Christmas carol,
filling up the silent night.

The Tree

How right and real the Christmas tree
that stands down in the town;
somehow it seemed more real and right
before they cut it down.

To be among the noted
you move off from the crowd.
As one small sapling in the wood
how can a tree feel proud?

But some trees, like some men,
take pride in staying where they are,
for greenness and reality
outshine the tinsel star.

from *Fields of Wonder*

Christ knows my span of concentration
and the time to teach me lessons
is the time when I'm boxed in by gray.
For when the sun shines,
what man fears God
or His one-begotten Son.
But Christ knows too
that He is always there
whatever time of year or day
more real for me
than what folks call reality.

Conscience

The wood holds dangers
darker than the dentist's chair
love is still the eye
of anything worthwhile
 or worth having
and so we keep that one eye open.

And knowing that it goes by
multitudes of attitudes and names
it's wise to learn and not forget
the favorite name for love is conscience.

Conscience being the first thing
Christ conceived for us
must mean love is Christmas
by another name.

bethlehem b.c.

You could hear
the flapping of their wings
for some distance—
not a sudden rush
        or a panic made by masses,
but a slow coming together
quietly in the air.

Then following that yellow highway
that the star provided,
into Bethlehem they came.
Slowly. Slowly. Quietly,
like a snowfall making up its mind
before a winter downpour.

And winter it was.

On the ground
we huddled—first in awe,
        then in fright—
thinking it miracle enough
that our important lives
should be interrupted
by creatures on a winter's eve
that flew above us, and beyond us,
to settle in the barnyard
        at the other end of town.

(We make up miracles to suit ourselves
and so we know these winged persons
had been sent for our amazement—
and not to please the cattle
in an unremembered farmer's barn.)

Were you there?

But file into the barn they did,
while some kept vanguard in the air
as though imagining they guarded
some important person
living there.

Some of us went home,
having seen them with no ill effect.
In the morning there'd be stores to open,
pigs to feed
and stories to enlarge upon
concerning what had happened
on the night before.

Were you there?

For My Son at Christmas

When Christmas comes around this year, I'd like to give you something that you least expect: your father's wisdom. If, indeed, he has yet acquired enough to share. Your father's charity, if he can truly say he has done nothing all these years to harm his fellow man. Your father's understanding, if he understands your needs well enough to listen to whole paragraphs of your young troubles without judging you in mid-sentence. Your father's absolution, though he himself has yet to be absolved for the recklessness he's passed down to you both knowingly and unknowingly. Your father's future, if he can see untroubled days ahead. Your father's needs, that you might meet the ones he never filled himself.

I hope, though, that your father, your old man, is not so selfish as to burden you with his unanswered prayers. Perhaps, after all, he'd better leave it to God to answer some of those requests you're making and will yet make up.

For Jean-Marc

May your life
be full for Christmas
this year and the next year too.
May the star that shines above us
always be there just for you.

And may your life
be bright and jolly.
Even when there is
no holly wreath to decorate the door
may the Christ of Christmas
help us love each other more.

May your hand be full for always
if only with another hand.
May your heart be empty only
long enough to give you cause
to fill it up again with love.

May your soul be lost by you
only to be found by God.

For You

I know love
by its first name
and living by its last.
I'm not afraid
of what's upcoming
or what has gone before
and if there's nothing left
to know about or learn
I'll review the early lessons
yet one more time.

Happy Christmas once again
and as we move
toward another year
may each day of it
bring all the love
            and friendship
your life needs.

True Holly

Because I love the sound of bells
I haunt the churchyards all year long
no matter where I might be traveling.

Because true holly makes me smile
I wait for Christmas just like children,
and I wait for Children too.

Because September travels slow
I catch it when I can
and hold it over for another month or so.

Because this year I'm poor again
I've written you another Christmas poem
made with last year's love and next year's too.

Because without God time is nothing,
I wish you time enough for everything
And God to help you regulate your hours.

Silent Knight, I

We're told He never cried
within the confines
of that ill-kept stable
on that dark and silent night
leaving even singing
       to the hosts.
Who but the Son of God
would miss the chance
to lift His voice
amid the angels?

Silent Knight, II

He must have been the Son of God.
What other man would take
                such chances?
None of any sanity,
and He had sanity to spare.
No magician He
for all the miracles
that He performed
were for the profit
of receivers only.

Can you imagine what
the doctor's fee might be
for healing lameness
                with a smile
and blindness with a wink?

And those mercenary merchants
would have jailed a man
far sooner than they did
the living, walking Christ
for turning water into wine.
Or making one thin slice of bread
                manna for the many.

Christmas Card

Where do they go
the people in our lives
who sail in like green leaves
and disappear like snow?
Not just in December
or the stormy winter months
but through the year and
through the years.

Looking up a name today
I passed through three pages of G's
and found at least six names
I can't remember or never knew.
I addressed and sent Christmas cards
out and over to them all the same
for what if someone
          somewhere else
fingering his phone book
passed over those same names.

Happy Christmas G's and X Y Z's
and thank you for whatever care
or kindness you passed along to me
that my addled brain forgot.

You I remember
because of what you are
               to me.
Merry Christmas.

Sweet Season

*Here in
the California winter
a mile away from snow
we hike down through
the holidays happily
but not so hurriedly
that we forget
our friends who celebrate
this same sweet season
beneath the southern sun.*

*And may we never
          once forget
the birthday of God's Son.*

*Good God give us more
than just our daily bread.
Pride in what we do for you,
hope for every new tomorrow,
love for all things living.
And as we forage in the new year
let our foraging be done
          in your name only.*

Make the songs we sing
songs of praise
            and not of glory
God of our fathers
be the one our singing turns to
as this Christmas passes
                    into history.

So My Sheep May Safely Graze
(Carol for Children)

So my sheep may safely graze
I climb the highest hill
and keep a watch out for the hawk
and the howling wolf.
I made a friend out of the wind
and got to know the snow
so even in the wintertime
my sheep may safely graze.

Calling, "Come sheep, come
I'll count you one by one,
one for John and one for Jacob
one for Job and one
for the child who's born this morning
in Bethlehem."

All good shepherds watch their flock
to the lowest lamb
so that they may safely graze
and never come to harm.
Guarded from the hunter's horn
shielded from the sun
all my sheep may safely graze
in far fields or at home.

Calling, "Come sheep, come
I'll count you one by one,
one for John and one for Jacob
one for Job and one
for the child who's born this morning
in Bethlehem."

Last night there were soldiers
on the road below the town
and creatures in the heavens
with wings of shiny gold.
One of them came close to me
saying, "Do not be afraid
a child of God was born this night
your sheep may safely graze."

Calling, "Come sheep, come
I'll count you one by one,
one for John and one for Jacob
one for Job and one
for the child who's born this morning
in Bethlemen."

SOME BASIC
QUESTIONS

Don't be chained by your beliefs; be
liberated by them.

Is belief in God enough?

It is not enough to believe God exists, nor even enough to respect Him as we respect our earthly parents. It is not enough to worship Him through some formal ritual. He asks that we serve Him, work for Him, dedicate our lives to furthering His kingdom on earth, and prepare ourselves for His invisible kingdom on the other side of this life. Belief is only the beginning. It is the life that counts.

Which God is the true God?

Though called by different names, and spoken of and defined by different doctrines, the God of all faiths is the same guiding force and deserves the same respect as the God you and I pray to.

Is there a path to follow?

I believe that in choosing a path, we must always choose the most challenging and difficult one. The easy road is crowded, and boring in the bargain. You will grow more if you attempt to travel with giants.

What is my responsibility in life?

My education and re-education in the ways of Christ, to better enable me to serve God through service to my brothers and sisters. Whenever theology is discussed, too little emphasis is placed upon the family of man. Even if it has become a cliché, the fact remains: you cannot have the father-hood of God without acknowledging the brother-hood and sisterhood of all human beings.

Why should I read the Bible?

The Scriptures contain all the most important ideas, thoughts, and master plans for those of us who wish to come closer to God. While people will always read into the Scriptures what they them-selves need to hear, perhaps that is as it should be. Any book as complex and complicated as the Bible is open to many kinds of interpretations. It would be nice, however, if some of us stopped dwelling on the fire and brimstone aspect of the Bible and spent more time reading, re-reading, and practic-ing the good and more positive thoughts to be found there.

But don't parts of the Bible seem strange, irrelevant, and unworkable?

Yes, and they also seem to be the ones cited, used, and rearranged by those who preach one thing for themselves and something else for their distressed and needing brothers and sisters. Chapter 21 of Leviticus contains two verses, one after the other, that offer a good illustration. The first will make you smile, and the second will certainly make you think:

5. They shall not make baldness upon their head, neither shall they shave off the corner of their beard nor make any cuttings in their flesh.
6. They shall be holy unto their God and not profane the name of their God: for the offerings of the Lord made by fire, and the bread of their God, they do offer: therefore they shall be holy.

I worry about my brothers who remain beardless after reading Verse 5. As for Verse 6, if you study it at length, it makes great sense and is the basis for more than one of the commandments sent down by God. Still, without any doubt, the Bible contains the rules for the best, and most exciting, life we can hope for.

Any particular favorites?

Many. What makes the Bible exciting is that you can open it almost anywhere and find something informative or incisive or just plain beautiful to read. That and the instructions it gives us are probably what set it apart from all other books. I love the Psalms, read as a whole or individually. For sheer poetry, the sections of the Old Testament dealing with the creation are magnificent in their language and accountability. But if I had to choose between the Old Testament and the New, I suppose I would favor the latter. It is a concise version of the book as a whole, and vivid in its depictions of Christ.

What about the so-called wrath of God?

Certainly it exists. If we go against God's principles—especially after we come to know them, if we break His commandments or fail to distinguish between right and wrong, we can expect God's displeasure. Fortunately for us, however, God doesn't carry grudges. We've only to be genuinely sorry for our sins and ask His forgiveness. That is one of the best things about following the teachings of Christ—knowing that God is a forgiving God.

What about the term "God-fearing?"

It is not meant to be taken literally. God gives us no reason whatsoever to fear Him—on the contrary, we should fear *not* being at one with God, since His is the only true way for us to find salvation. To be God-fearing is to acknowledge Him as the creator of all things and, therefore, the key to all the mysteries of the universe. We are fortunate that he asks us to join in a partnership with Him in the upkeep of what He has already made and continues to create. To know God and to know His love is to be God-fearing.

Do Christians have any fun?

You bet. God wants us to have good, healthy, and loving relationships with each other. The secret is to be positive, outgoing, and giving. We should always give love, not just expect to receive it. In coming to earth, Christ showed us that.

God wants us to be positive in everything we undertake, and that includes any pursuit that calls for change or choice. We should always be courageous and caring.

ACKNOWLEDGMENTS

The poem "An Outstretched Hand" was written and dedicated to Jay Allen in 1968. It was published that same year in *Lonesome Cities*, a Random House/Cheval Book, copyright © 1968 by Rod McKuen. It has since been used for fund-raising activities by The American Cancer Society, The March of Dimes, UNESCO, The National Heart Foundation, The Children's Fund, and Animal Concern, among others.

"Flying in the Face of God" is from *Come to Me in Silence*, published by Simon & Schuster and Cheval Books, copyright © 1973 by Montcalm Productions and Rod McKuen.

"And to Each Season," "So My Sheep May Safely Graze," "In Order of Importance," "For Jean-Marc," "Conscience," "The Lovers of December," and "The Singer and the Song" are from *The Carols of Christmas*, published by Random House and Cheval Books, copyright © 1970, 1971, 1980 by Rod McKuen and Montcalm Productions.

"For You," "The Green," "Celebrate," "Seeds," "Boundaries," "Runner," "Earth," "Assessment,"

About the Author

Rod McKuen's books of poetry have sold more than 20 million copies in hardcover. Among them are *Stanyan Street and Other Sorrows, Listen to the Warm, Moment to Moment, Celebrations of the Heart,* and *We Touch the Sky.* His film music has twice been nominated for an Academy Award ("The Prime of Miss Jean Brodie" and "A Boy Named Charlie Brown"); and in 1973 a suite entitled "The City," commissioned and performed by the Louisville Orchestra, was nominated for a Pulitzer Prize in music. He has received the Horatio Alger, Carl Sandburg, and Walt Whitman Awards and medals from the Freedoms Foundation, and his book *Finding My Father,* about the search for his natural father, has helped to change adoption- and access-to-information laws in nearly a dozen states.

Mr. McKuen's other classical music consists of symphonies, several suites and ballets, and a full-length opera, "The Black Eagle." Among his popular songs are "Jean," "Rock Gently," "A Boy Named Charlie Brown," "Love's Been Good to Me," "If You Go Away," and "Seasons in the Sun." They have been translated into more than forty languages. His concerts worldwide are automatic sellouts.

Before emerging into the limelight as a best-selling author and composer, Mr. McKuen was a laborer, cowboy, rodeo rider, shoe salesman, lumberjack, doorman at a movie theater, and radio disc jockey, among a dozen or more varied occupations. He also spent two years in the Army, during and after the Korean War.

In addition to *An Outstretched Hand* the author will have two other books published this year—a collection of love poetry entitled *Finding a Friend* and an extensive book about America, *The Power Bright and Shining.*

Mr. McKuen's permanent residence is a rambling Spanish house in southern California, which he shares with a menagerie of Old English sheepdogs and a number of cats.